AF591414

THE DEVIL, His Demons, And the fight for our souls.

An Anthology of
Inspiring
Essays

Hugh J. Harmon

THE DEVIL, His Demons and the fight for our souls

By Hugh J. Harmon

THE DEVIL, His Demons and the fight for our souls

Copyright © 2010 by Hugh J. Harmon. All rights reserved. No part of this book may be used or reproduced in any manner whatsoever without written permission of the publisher, except in the case of brief quotations in articles and reviews. For information write: Kingdom Book & Gift LLP., PO Box 291975, Columbia SC 29229.

ISBN-13 978-0-557-88936-5

Unless otherwise noted, all Scripture quoted is from the KJV.

Printed in the United States of America

Please visit our website for other great titles:
http://www.wix.com/trends/kingdombookandgift

For information regarding author interviews, please contact the publicity department via email:
Kingdombookandgift@gmail.com

KB&G

Kingdom Book & Gift LLP
Publishers and Booksellers

Contents

Introduction

When we consider the ensuing conflict for world dominion, political unrest, religious persecution, widespread outbreaks of disease, catastrophic natural disasters, economic upheaval of a global scale, the general eroding of traditional values and the diminishing of morality to its lowest denominator called relativism, the obvious conclusion is that life as we know it is in the throes of a state of confusion bordering on chaos. What a profoundly matter-of-fact statement to make, one must be saying! These issues, be it political posturing, religious schisms, disease outbreaks, natural disasters, economic downturns or just the challenges facing a society where lawlessness seems to be looming larger than common decency, some would argue, have always been a part of the unfolding drama of life in the civilized world. As soon as man had developed the wherewithal to organize systems of governance and decided that he would settle and adopt or make an identity for himself the questions and the challenges that these arrangements have created throughout history has led us to experience these difficult times and circumstances. However, the astute scholar of human history would also be remised to not point out that despite the evidence of these aforementioned issues being always a part of human existence, they have never quite been beset upon us all at the same time and with such intensity as they are today.

When we think about the gravity of our dire straits or we attempt to give meaning to our condition or our current state of affairs, we must always keep in mind that there are a multiplicity of perspectives as to what is going on, if anything out of the ordinary is taking place, and whether action steps have to be taken to somehow remedy what is out of sync or alignment. The debate then turns into the fact that some people will not see anything extraordinarily awry, and that there are others who will say that what is being sensed is dependent upon the individual's perspective and worldview. In this essay, or commentary from a spiritual perspective, I would like to suggests a biblical worldview of the conflicts and the perceived crises. First, I would propose that my contention is that something is awry, but not some anomaly that we must be afraid of, but rather I think that we should adopt a posture of alarm, anticipation and preparation for the unfolding of some great truths, and prophetic promises that were spoken of centuries and even millennia before our time that we are fortunate enough to be the latter day beneficiaries of their tangible manifestation. Yes, this essay is written from Christian worldview, and I am unapologetic about my convictions. Some may immediately dismiss the precepts contained within this publication because they ascribe to another faith. However, I challenge you despite your background, the beliefs you currently adhere to, or your desire to remain neutral in the often referenced "wars over religion" to take some time and reason together with me as I deal with the subject of "***The Devil, his de-***

mons and the fight for our souls."

The title alone may have created some apprehension in you because even in Christian circles there is both debate and apprehension over the nature, operation and/or relevance of demonic activity in the life of the faithful. Much of contemporary Christianity has become more of an indictment of man's frailties, faults and self-imposed hindrances than any outright condemnation of a real, tangible, existing enemy. Nevertheless, I am from both a faith tradition within the camp of Christianity, and from a cultural background that has always recognized the necessity for acknowledging the existence of dark forces around us. Therefore, we must understand by inference that the evil and its agency is not just a

Judeo-Christian concept but rather has universal implications. Throughout my life, I have been taught that we have a real enemy, with really critical intentions when it comes to my life, my families life and the disruption of my peace, safety and comfort in this world. As I have grown in my Christian faith I have come to give that enemy a name or a nomenclature and that is, the devil.

The Devil, his demons, and the fight for our souls is my minor attempt under the inspiration of the Holy Spirit to address the enemy, his agents and what I believe to be the most urgent conflict that we may be engaged in as humans in a scarred and fallen world. I have to preface this attempt and say that it is not like my previous endeavors where I attempted to articulate the depths of my biblical study on a particular scriptural or doctrinal principle and to the best of my ability with God's assistance presented in a tutorial type of presentation that one may be able to go and spark great conversation, and come to a greater knowledge of their personal walk with God. Rather, in this book, which is really an extended thought on an issue that is of great personal importance, I am not attempting to teach, preach or prognosticate but rather I am simply speaking my mind.

If you have not figured it out yet, you soon will understand that much of what we posit as faith and our belief is harvested from our thoughts that are shaped, molded and defined by our experiences.

These really and truly can never ever wholly mirror someone else's because we look at our own life through our own lenses, and the journey of the images from before our eyes, to when they are processed on the visual sensors of our eyes after having been siphoned through the cognitive mechanisms of our mind often looks totally different from person to person. So I ask you to bear with me, as I make some suppositions and suggests some ways of thinking about life's difficulties and how we may overcome them, and know that you have the right to disagree. However, I don't think you have the right to stay neutral. C.S. Lewis, the late great Christian thinker, theologian and author once said, and I wholeheartedly concur and agree, "There is no neutral ground in the universe: every square inch, every split second is claimed by God and counterclaimed by Satan." Why don't you stake your claim and make your destiny a sure thing?

Essay One

The Confrontation

"A man cannot by the craft and flattery of his tongue lay hold of God while his heart is far away. No, for since God is spirit and truth, a man can only draw near to Him by sincerity, by willing to be holy, as He is holy, by purity of heart."

Soren Kierkegaard

We must begin where it counts, and make our beginning count. It troubles me adversely when I meet people who speak with great anxiety, hurriedly trying to explain where they are going tomorrow, or by next year, or by ten years from now and then they step out with trepidation or stand still riddled with angst. They make great attempts at starting where it counts but their start never counts because they actually miss what really counted. Before we can move forward in thought, word or deed we have to confront ourselves. That's it, I said it, you thought I was going to say confront your enemy, the devil, but no, there I said it, your first assignment is really to confront you. And in the confrontation hit where it will count, and that is in your heart. The Bible teaches us, implores us in Proverbs 4:23, "Keep thy heart with all diligence; for out of it are the issues of life." In the New Living Translation of the Bible, the translators turned it up a notch in that same scripture verse and said it like this, "Guard your heart above all else, for it determines the course of your life." So when we are thinking where should we begin, and in beginning making sure that it counts our most challenging place is in our own heart, above all else. Before we consider our bellies: fulfilling our appetites, our leanings and proclivities, we must go to the source within us that is our hearts. It is the clearinghouse, the place where stuff gets stamped and approved for distribution and dispersal about the body.

How do I confront my heart? How do I start

to make changes in an organ that has such great importance in my basic survival? How can I confront and potentially bring to a grinding halt work in a place whose work keeps me alive? To confront is to face down, it is point out that which disturbs you or threatens your wellbeing or progress. It is to vigorously debate your position in order to get the other party to see, or at least respect your position. I can't possibly do that with my own heart because then I will be revolting against me. Now here is where it gets tricky, because that revolt by me and in me is the battle that determines my destiny. Putting you on blast, making you see you for who you really are, and not what you have been living your entire life trying to portray you to be.

To better understand the predicament that has befallen us, we must better understand us. To better understand us, which may appear to be a task that is out of our reach, we have to look to God. For man to fully understand God is as if Sherlock Holmes and Dr. Watson were astute enough, clever enough, and intellectually prodigious enough to solve the mystery of who was Sir Arthur Conan Doyle. For some of you that statement makes no sense, because you have a passing knowledge of Sherlock Holmes and Dr. Watson, the famed British detective and his trusty companion, but many of you have no idea who Sir Arthur Conan Doyle is, but you should know quite simply he is the author and creator of the fictional characters and hugely popular series of books on their escapades and adventures as detectives solving crimes in the gritty communities of turn-of-the-century London. When I say we have to look to God to better understand us, I do not mean that we have to fully understand Him because that is an impossible and insurmountable task. But rather we have to look to what He said concerning man and how His relationship, as according to scripture, demonstrates his unfolding relationship with man.

When man appears in God's divine purview as described by scripture, and if we were to stick primarily to the chronological development of it all we would see that man was mentioned quite some time after much of creation was completed. However, this chronological approach does not do us justice because further on in scripture we hear, deduce and can tacitly conclude that man was actually on God's mind first and creation was built with the intent of being within the extent purposes of human invention and within the primary purposes of God. In other words, man wasn't made for the world, the world was made for man. Man came first in God's thoughts and the world is an outworking of God's original intentions toward man. Genesis 1:26 says, And God said, "Let us make man..." the subtle implication is that this declaration was the product of a forethought, not a new revelation that was birthed out of, or because of a perceived missing piece, but as the next piece in an unfolding puzzle that God had already seen completed.

The Bible also teaches us in subsequent text not given attention in the Genesis scriptures but relevant to our understanding of them, that man was created to fulfill God's good pleasure. Paul the apostle to the gentiles in addressing the church at Ephesus made a strong statement about God and where His mind was concerning His people. "According as he has chosen us in him before the foundation of the world,...Having predestinated us unto the adoption..., according to the good pleasure of his will." Two statements in those two abbreviated verses stand out to me, before the foundation, and predestinated. Before the foundation is speaking about prior to the substance upon which the very world subsists and exists was put down, God chose not just place you but simply to make you. Predestinated means that He saw your destination in advance of your destination even being created.

God was and is God all by Himself. He is all-sufficient and does not need anything, anyone or any ideology to validate Him. However, He sought pleasure in making man, and the world that He would eventually place man in supplied with all that He needed, and wanted, and He also gave man responsibility and value in the process. When we look at the dynamic between expecting parents and the idea of a pending child in the natural this concept becomes more clear. As expectant parents we make plans for the arrival of a healthy girl or boy. We may look into getting a larger residence so that we can facilitate the new need for space. We purchase or ask for donations and gifts of baby furniture. We buy clothes and bed linens and blankets to assure that when this child arrives that they would never suffer the pain or affects of cold temperatures in the atmosphere. We obtain baby formulas, or the mother prepares to breastfeed. We paint, we decorate, we get ready for this child to arrive. And when they do arrive they immediately partake of what we have prepared. But also in the process we teach the baby to recognize people. They learn who Daddy is even if they don't understand. They learn who Mommy is even if they don't understand. They get toys and teddy bears and such and these too are devices that are bought to help make this child comfortable in new surroundings. However, as time goes on we as parents need to teach this child their name, and give them the independence to recognize that the room we decorated, painted and placed mobiles on the wall of, and portraits on the banister of is really their room. Even with children we move from all out support and provision to them taking ownership for things they didn't and couldn't purchase for themselves but they use daily. It is for our good pleasure as parents and for our peace of mind that we buy these things for our children and they in turn use these things and down the road will take ownership of them and responsibility for them.

Beginning where it counts begins in the human heart, and knowing that we owe ourselves better and that when we started out we were in a much better condition than we are in right now, and we are where we are right now because we made some poor choices, made some choices during seasons of transition that ultimately became destiny decisions, and downright failed to follow the instructions. The confrontation is in you. It is the facing of the enemy on the inside of you, because it is that enemy that gets you into relationship with the subject of this book-the enemy of our souls, the devil.

The devil does not enter in, where he does not feel welcome, or where he is not given an invitation. He only comes in where he fits in. The Bible says in the book of Ephesians and the fourth chapter of that book, "Neither give place to the devil." Place here should really be translated and interpreted, opportunity. When it says give no place, we must understand that this means it is within our power to erect barriers in our life to keep the evil one out. It tells us that we are equipped with enough rigor to keep the devil at bay. As believers, as the faithful, we must remember or I must interject that this textual reference in Ephesians was addressing Christians. Non-Christians are not equipped or capacitated with the ability to do this. Please understand that this edict by Paul is the sole privilege of believers and those that are continually pursuing God. If we look at the account of the fall of man in the book of Genesis we see clear evidence of this very principle being worked out. Adam and Eve, created and existing in communion with God. It seems almost immediately that what God had created in perfection, and what he had dubbed to be very good was so rapidly perverted and plagued with the sickness of sin. But the Bible is deliberate in that it does not ascribe lengths of time to this garden sojourn of the first man and woman. We just know that one day a rebel didn't even just show up, but a rebel began to speak. This rebel defined as the serpent of guile began to speak. I call him a rebel because his first words are words of sedition and deception. All the words spoken prior to this that were publicly spoken and recorded in Holy Writ were words that were either creative, supportive, empowering or naming. But for the first time we have words that question the heart and the intent of the creator. It was not just that these words were questioning and crouched in evoking doubt but the tragedy was that these words were directed at undermining the creator. Always know that ultimately, at the heart of the matter, the devil is not targeting you because he ostensibly does not fear you, but is really leveling his attacks at God and the host in heaven that stood their ground when he initiated an insurrection there. He does envy you, and he does hold a grudge because in us he sees what he feels can be fodder to use against God and to accuse God of injustice. What do I mean by this? What was the devil's charge in heaven? It was the indictment handed down which read accusation pride and self-centeredness. He was ejected from heaven and a third of the angels that followed him, and wanted to be a part of his entourage because pride in self made him augment his purpose, which was to lead in God's praise. He turned around and saw all the other angel's praising, following his able-leading and thought that it would be great for him to receive such reverence. He moved from being the worship leader to having the deep desire to be worshiped. The devil's argument since then has been that man when he fell did the same thing that he did as an angel but God continues to give man a second chance and he did not get a second chance. This is why the devil feels that he has some morsel of error that he can bring against God. But this devil we learn later on through careful study of scripture actually possesses the body of a serpent and injects words riddled with strife and contention into the atmosphere of the garden of Eden. The Bible does not say that the serpent came along one day, it does not say that Adam and Eve were walking along a street that they had never been down before. It simply says the serpent started speaking. And the dangerous next step is that man started to listen. They didn't just hear the serpent speaking they heard, heeded, and hearkened onto the voice. That speech engaged an action in them that gave place to the devil to speak some more and to watch what happens.

Hopefully you followed the chain of that thought and you arrived here at the same place that I am, in realizing that Adam and Eve weren't finagled arm-twisted, coaxed or tortured into eating the fruit that God forbade them to eat, but they were moved by a word and that word was only able to move them because it found a familiar place in them. Look at how it unfolded. *And when the woman saw that the tree was good for food* (Genesis 3:6a), it didn't say after the serpent took her head and shoved it upon the fruit. It said she saw, she came to a revelation of sorts on her own that what God had forbid even touching was not just good to touch but was even better to eat and consume. How often do we fly in the face of God and tell Him that what he is requiring of us in His word is too hard for us and we know a better way. Or even more realistic and poignant are the times when we eat, partake of, and consume physically or mentally what God simply told us we could not, and it was because of the implication that it was no good for us. *And when the woman saw...that it was pleasant to the eyes,* (Genesis 3:6b), this suggests that because of the divine prohibition communicated to Adam the communication from husband to wife had gone to the level where Eve feared to even look at the fruit of the tree of the knowledge of good and evil. The prohibition had done two related things in Eve. It had caused her to create in her mind an image of the fruit that was ugly. And this image had served to aid reinforcing her commitment to not even look at the fruit. But this exercise in suppositions and assumptions on her part also created a curiosity and fascination with the fruit of this tree. This predisposition was what connected with the serpent's words and engendered action on her part. *And when the woman saw...a tree to be desired to make one wise she took of the fruit thereof* (Genesis 3:6c), the last straw was that she had something in her that relished wisdom. For some reason she thought that what she knew already was not enough and that the prohibition was God's way of keeping her from attaining to some great knowledge that could possibly improve her lot better than what it already was, free, possessing all, having all dominion and enabled to reproduce and multiply. The word wise here is the Hebrew word, sakal. It means to make or to cause to be circumspect, to be intelligent and not just in the cursory sense but to become an expert at, to have good success, to prosper and to guide wittingly. Eve somehow became the victim of the serpent's words and was driven to believe either initially or as a result of those words, that she was either not intelligent, intelligent enough or being blocked by God from becoming like Him. The key is not whether her thoughts were true or not, it is more important that we see the motivation behind her action is the really condemnation. The suggestion is that God does not have your best interest at heart and that you have to somehow circumvent God to get the best that you should have out of life.

The confrontation is about upbraiding all of you that thinks wrongly about God and what God wants for you. As of late my motto, my personal motivational statement has been, "How are you seeing God today?" What does he look like? That question or statement has several layers to it. When I say see God I mean what place does he have in your life. And also I mean how do you assess his ability to make a difference in your life. When you get a right view, a right image, a holistic perspective of God you will better be able to know what you should be expecting in life, what you should be rejecting from having entrance into your life and what you should be inviting to take up residence in your life. I can judge God correctly if my eye is filled with the plank of my own error, because I am then judging God's sufficiency and God's ability from a deficient point of view to begin with.

I am to blame. We are to blame. I am responsible, and we are responsible for where we are today to the extent that we got here because we made conscious decisions based in unconscious deception that let to faulty perception. And if we continue to trust in our faulty perception to bring about necessary change we will remain on the cul-de-sac to nowhere, trusting in nothing that is dressed up like something, heading nowhere that is disguised as a destination and only to find out that it is a prop like that used in sitcoms and soap operas not worth the siding and vinyl upon which it is painted an propped upon to give the illusion of reality.

If I am to blame for my condition, and the

devil's words are just the incinerating, flammable device that is laid to the combustible material of our misdirected lives, I have to take steps to eradicate my life of thinking, attitudes, behaviors and mindsets that have demonic origin. The devil is called the "accuser of the brethren", (Revelation 12:10). That is what he has become as of late but his original accusation was laid squarely at the foot of the throne of heaven. The devil is an accuser of God before the people of God. From words of enticement to rebel such as, "God didn't really say that, to God will never get you out of that, to God can't forgive you of that, to God is not hearing your prayers, to God is preventing you from experiencing real liberty, to following God is more bondage than living in sin."

He is now fully employed and has his agents employed in accusing you before God because he has realized that God cannot and will not be moved, shaken or disturbed. But he sure can bug the warts out of you. He knows what buttons to hit, and what doubts to stoke, and what anxieties to fire up in us. But just as the devil knows how to get us going, God has equipped us with power or at least access to power to cut his legs off at the pass. We have the ability in our sanctified, born-again lives to silence the enemy of our souls, but before we can do it we have to put ourselves in check. Paul at his wits end trying to walk this life of faith out as best he knew how, while not constricting himself to the rigid confines of legalism that he had been raised and indoctrinated to revere and respect highly cried out in his epistle to the church at Rome. He was correcting them in the error of returning to a law-led life. He wasn't talking about living outside of the law, being lawless and believing in relativism as some would take it today but rather he was talking about living as slaves to ritual and religion, and living almost a permanently punished existence. After Paul exhorted to them that he understood the struggle, wanting to do right and having the penchant for doing the opposite, he says, "O wretched man that I am! Who shall deliver me from the body of this death?" (Romans 7:24) And he answers just as resoundingly his own question, "I thank God through Jesus Christ our Lord." He acknowledged that he was a wretch. The word that was translated wretch here is the same Hebrew term for adulterer or apostate. Paul said I find that in me, I have the desire to make other things god in my life. I have the propensity of having God in the fore-front of my mind but also holding onto other people, experiences, and ideas in reserve. And some of those other people, experiences and ideas serve to satisfy in me the same things that I seek God for. That was the sin of Eve. She saw in the fruit fulfillment of the same needs and wants that she had been seen filled by God-food, pleasure and wisdom.

For the confrontation to conclude with results, in order that we can make our beginning count we have to do some metaphorical "spring cleaning". And this is not some simple dusting of the shelves, replacing the batteries in the smoke detector, vacuuming and shampooing the carpets and maybe scrubbing out the tub and shower but this requires some whole scale dumping of rubbish and that which is in disrepair. I would even challenge you to not have a garage sale but neatly package it and put in a pile next to the road where it is easily visible by the garbage disposal team as they drive through your neighborhood. For this confrontation to work we have to just get rid of that which is of the devil and does not find its origin in God, and don't attempt to garner any profit from what you cast out. Don't sell it in yard sale and don't even give it away, throw by the side of the road with the intention of it being garbage.

Sincerity, having a willingness to be holy and desiring the right heart are the keys to defeating evil in our lives. And when we defeat evil in our lives we are better able to hear God, touch God, communicate with God and more clearly receive instruction and direction from Him. David the shepherd boy that became the celebrated King of Israel, knew both what it was to be connected to God, hearing continually from God and to feel that God was a thousand miles away on other business. It was because he had lived at times locked into God and doing precisely what he said, and at other times he attempted to navigate through his personal setbacks his own way. David penned the fifty-first Psalm in which he said, "Create in me a clean heart, O God; and renew a right spirit within me. Cast me not away from thy presence; and take not thy holy spirit from me. Restore unto me the joy of thy salvation…" We hear here, the heart of a man that was drenched in contradiction. He loved God, wanted to do right by God but had also come to a clear realization that there was a part of himself that was in dangerous territory and he could lose it all, and he needed help. That's our story, we need help, and at times in our lives we are on fire for Jesus walking in the middle of the narrow road of holiness and other times we are transported to the broad way of sin and we like it, and to be honest we don't know how to fix it. The fixing begins with renouncing some things. As lords, and kings, and priest we are afforded not only the external trappings of those titles like the robes, the rings and the crowns but we are more so afforded the authority to announce that some things are no longer legally or legitimately welcome into our territory. Join me as I kick off this recruitment effort and this orientation into basic training and lets make some renouncements. Imagine that your party has just won the elections and you have just been handed a pen as the President or the leader of your known world, and you have veto power to rewrite the laws. The Bible says that the Word is nigh thee, even in thy mouth, and in thy heart: that is the word of faith, which we preach, that if thou shalt confess with thy mouth the Lord Jesus, …" The power for your turnaround, and your defeat of the devil and his demons is to be found in the word. Your part and position; what you have been employed to do as an occupier for the kingdom in this battle for world dominion begins with what you say to the circumstances you face, the feelings that are resident inside you, and the naysayers that are arrayed against you.

In the confrontation this is my declaration:

God we begin by saying thank you for the simple endowment of life, health and strength. According to the forecast our condition may be that of debt, disease and limited strength. But we do not declare what we feel, see or are hearing from those around us, but rather we realize that as much as we may be in debt there are others who are debt free but do not have our joy, peace or hope; as much as we may be diseased in our bodies there are those who are as sick as us and have resolved that they will only get worse but your grace has given us the wherewithal to expect healing; as weak as we may be feeling today, relative to our neighbors who don't know you we have an abundance of strength for the joy of the Lord is my strength. God we appreciate your providence in good times and in the bad. Today, we take a bold step to cast off and lock out all that is contrary to your will and your way in my life. There are things that I have to exterminate, expel, and eradicate out of my life in order that I may advance to the finish. God renew a right spirit within me. Create in me a clean heart. Cast not thy Holy Spirit from me Lord.

I repent today. I seek your forgiveness today. I have fallen short again and I need your help to cancel the devil's assignment over my life. I acknowledge these sins, I put a name to them and the spotlight of the Lord's Word and truth upon them. I separate them from my life in the name of Jesus. I renounce all....

Pride	*Greed*
Jealousy	*Envy*
Unnatural Affections	*Bad Habits*
Regret	*Anger*
Hatred	*Unforgiveness*
Vengefulness	*Strife*
Deceit	*Lying*
Accusatory Spirit	*Blaming Spirit*
Lust of the Flesh	*Perverted Thinking*
Uncleanness	*Impurity*
Sexual sin	*Evil Speech*

Gossip *Immorality*

Unrepentance

God as you remove these things that afflict I thank you for affixing in their place, the direct opposites.

Contentment *Joy*

Soberness *Sound thinking*

Peace *Fellowship*

Encouragement *Natural affections*

Pleasing thoughts *Humility*

Hope *Sense of Achievement*

Self-Control *Truthfulness*

Desire to make peace

By the power of His blood and according to His mighty hand and most excellent name, Jesus the Christ, it is done and accomplished in the Earth, and in my circum-

stances as it is in Heaven.

Essay Two

The Threat

"The atheist can't find God and relishes his ignorance of him for the same reason that a thief can't find a policeman and enjoys the company of darkness."

"Now the serpent was more subtil than any beast of the field which the Lord God had made."

Genesis 3:4

"How art thou fallen from heaven, O Lucifer, son of the morning! How are thou cut down to the ground, which didst weaken the nations!"

Isaiah 14:12

"Thine heart was lifted up because of thy beauty, thou hast corrupted thy wisdom by reason of thy brightness: I will cast thee to the ground, I will lay thee before kings, that they may behold thee."

Ezekiel 28:17

"And He (Jesus) said unto them, "I beheld Satan as lightning fall from heaven."

Luke 10:18

The Bible declares that by the mouth of two or three witnesses every word is established. The principle that this scripture postulates is that in the court of divine counsel, repetition two to three times by varying witnesses serves as enough qualification for the veracity of a spoken word of God. In other words, if the same testimony-remarks or language espoused by two to three witnesses concurs and agrees they establish a Divinely corroborated truth. The question is whether the devil exists. The devil, sin, the distinctions between right and wrong, morality, ethics, the separation of church and state, the legalizing of abortion, the redefinition of marriage, these are all topics that some years ago were danced around in public debates and conversations, but today they have become the acceptable course of consumption on our daily broadcast television talk shows and talk-radio programs. Media has slowly but surely brought these once taboo issues mainstream by slowly planting messages neatly between the scenarios in our situational comedy series and into the unfolding plots of our soap operas until they are now the scoop on the new current craze called reality T.V. In the political arena, the diplomatically savvy have legislated these activities and practices that were once thought of as obvious and clear demonstrations of sin at work, and brought them into the mainstream and the norm, by giving people the legal right to not only pursue what was once known as deviant lifestyles, but to lobby for greater freedoms to engage in such, and the right to prosecute those that object.

In the details of this whole charade of sorts is the devil. You know how we always said, "It's the devil in the details!" We are literally seeing that simple proverb proven time and time again. Lawyers, legislators and activists judges with the liberty of pen and the freedom of speech ransacking the details of this country's constitution and more importantly the constitution of heaven, the Bible, to find ways to validate what they see as behaviors, lifestyle choices and attitudes that are perceived to be hindering the liberties of a growing faction of our community. The more the details of the Bible are squabbled over, the greater the effort becomes for some "to remove the landmarks" of our faith; the more the devil becomes this boogie man that is a figment of the human imagination. However, scripture tells us and assures us not only with the few verses I mentioned at the beginning of this text, but in many other places, about the existence of a real enemy, who goes by innumerable names, none two inviting, but who we will simply refer to as the devil.

The devil is real. He is not a production of the collective fears of mankind. He is not some psychological scapegoat that we have created to dump the blame for all of our issues, he, however, is a diabolical figure throughout human history. And as outrageous as it may seem for us to believe that, there is this one being that wreaks havoc on the nations as the Bible describes it, because we just can't see it in human terms, know that that problem can be easily explained. He, the devil is not human. I would not even describe him as super-human, I think the better term would be in-human, and by that I mean unlike human altogether.

The devil as he currently stands is the most menacing threat to humankind. It isn't nuclear disaster, it isn't global warming, it isn't catastrophic meteor fall out, but rather it is that the devil is loose, and some people still think that he does not exist. We are in a dangerous place in human history because the doctrine that espouses that there is no devil, no sin, no wrong, no deviance, just degrees of relative right is gaining steam. Like no other time it is becoming accepted truth. Any good military strategist will tell you that the most troublesome concern in waging war is not troop size, weapon capacity or even battle strategy, but rather the most important concern is knowing who your enemies are. War thrives on intelligence. In the tragic killing fields of Vietnam, America took major casualties because when they arrived in the mosquito infested battlegrounds known as rainforest in the Vietnam war they were ambushed time and time again due to guerilla warfare tactics in which civilian citizens who looked like allies were being employed by the enemy to take American GI's by surprise. They did not really know who their enemies were.

What is the real threat that we face as believers, as the faithful followers of Christ given the duty to occupy (take a militaristic stance) until He, our redeemer, returns? First of all, our number one threat issue is that we wouldn't blindly overlook the devil and get lulled into the same defeated mindset of the unbelieving world that all we are experiencing in this life is karma; when good goes out good comes back to you, and when bad goes out bad comes back to you. Jesus, in preaching and teaching about his purpose in coming to dwell among us, said some really poignant things that are directly relevant to this idea of whether the devil exist or not. Jesus said, "For the thief cometh but to steal, kill and destroy but I have come that you might have life and that more abundantly." Jesus used the analogy of burglary or pilfering, not to comment on burglary or stealing per se in the natural sense, but instead to illustrate the divisive tactics of the devil. He is like a thief, operating under the cover of darkness so that you can't easily detect his presence and then he pounces. Jesus is giving an illustration of how we may miss the devil and question his existence because we don't necessarily see him in the execution of the act. Statistics show that thieves are seldom observed in the act, it is the evidence that tells on them. It is the same way with the devil. Just because you didn't see Satan (i.e. the devils most popular common name) come into your home, influence your child, cause your spouse to backslide, and create ways to get at your finances it does not mean that he doesn't exist. The evidence of a broken marriage, a home filled with confusion, and finances that are always at a critical shortage especially when you want to do what God asked of you it is evidence of the devil and his poisoned touch.

The second threat that is injurious to our walk in Christ is the threat that he is something we don't need to worry about in the present scheme of things. Yes, the Bible is rife with chapters and verses where God continually assures the saints that Satan is no match for Him. Over and over again we are boldly encouraged to press on, believe God, don't give up now because the devil is already a defeated foe whose demise is set. But while saying that the Bible also tells us "to be careful for nothing but in everything with prayer and supplication make our request known unto God", "it says that we should walk circumspectly not as fools, but as wise," the wise are prudent in their ways because the days are evil. These text and many others teach us that we are living in the devil's day. It is a time when he is at his most powerful, exercising influence far and wide. We as believers have two simple duties, be watchful and stay in communication with God. When we watch and pray we become God's eyes and ears in the land. We become his intelligence source on the enemy. It is not that God doesn't know what he is up to, but God does it that way so that He can show unbelievers and those seeking to know Him what He is capable of. When Jesus was informed of Lazarus's sickness that was unto death he did something quite uncommon for someone who was a friend, and who potentially had the remedy to their friends illness. Jesus stood right where he was. He did not rush to Lazarus's bedside but actually went about doing some more miracles until the word came that Lazarus was dead. Then when Jesus did arrive and was about to go in and perform the even more awesome miracle of calling a dead man out of the grave he lifted his head, and He made a show of praying to the Father in Heaven. Then he commented that He was doing it not for himself, but rather that those who stood around mourning, expecting to move on with life without Lazarus could see that God had power over death as well. When people see us pray and get results in our lives in the midst of adverse situations and our lives are changed God gets the glory, the devil is defeated and we get the victory.

The third disconcerting threat that the devil brings against us is that of the resolution that if he does exist he is just the dark side of humans. He is just the extreme manifestation of our fears and all that could be bad about us. This suggestion I believe is swiftly unseated when we look at the gospel accounts of Jesus and his demonic encounters and what ensued in those meetings. First, there was the young man who would often throw himself in the fire and cut his flesh. They called him a lunatic. But when Jesus was summoned to do what His disciples had difficulty doing, the Bible says that Jesus rebuked the devil and he departed out of the boy. It was not just the boys evil side, it was something completely foreign to the boy and as I described earlier in-human because it had the ability to enter into the very body of humans and exist. The story concludes with this remark, "and the child was cured from that very hour." This issue was not just some bad seed, or some overt manifestation of all that was evil in the boy. It was a sickness. It was an infestation.

Another threat and one that undermines and maims the progress and potential of many believers is that of demonic distraction that makes us focus on the people in our lives that appear to be hindering us, rather than paying careful attention to how the devil may be the force behind the interruption of your peace. This is the threat of demonizing individuals rather than recognizing the real architect of your distress in your life. This is not some mystical argument where you rule out the fact that people just don't like you, and genuinely can't get along with you or your personality, and just develop this spiritual paranoia where you are looking for the devil in every remark or look. However, we must not also get wrapped up into emotional responses where we enter into anger and make statements that ultimately erode our witness because we are retaliating against people and not our real enemy. It is easy for us to get focused on the haves and the have nots. It is easy to see those who seem to have it out for you. But we must stay aware of the fact that people have no more power over you than you allow. Most of the time people that are hindering you have been deluded into thinking that you are their enemy. They have been made to somehow be convinced that you have something that belongs to them. They are often doing what they do out of some spite or slight that they believe you brought against them or that benefited you while been disadvantageous to them. Guess what? The devil is behind that misinformation. The misinformation that breeds racism, sexism and all forms of discrimination that has people believing that they are somehow better than some other faction of society based merely on biological or perceived economic differences is as a result of demonic misinformation. That misinformation is fueled or ignited in the fire of discontent. If my life does not add up, and I'm seemingly always on the short end of the stick and I'm taught from early on to look at those that are different from me with suspicion or hatred, I will inevitably develop a mindset that says that our differences are indicators of inferiority and necessitates division and conflict. If I see you as lower than me, and then I see you gaining some advantages in life that were once exclusively the right and privilege of my group, then I see your gains as a subordination of my status and actually the act of taking something for your possession that is rightfully mine. That is a classic example of demonic brainwashing that teaches that resources are limited and therefore belong to one group and the other group is not as valuable and therefore they do not have a right to or deserve access to those resources. The dog eat dog mentality has demonic roots.

The threats of the faithful are numerous. These are just a few of the ways that the devil weaves his web of deceit and literally leaves himself out of the picture. The more ways that he can accomplish to make you think that he is too incredible to be real, and Christians are just this paranoid, delusional group of ingrates, then he can continue to spawn his web of lies, lethargy and lunacy in the earth, and leave the saints believing that they are losing more than they are winning.

One other factor that is related to the devil, but is not under his direct control and is therefore not often seen as a threat is the issue of the proclivities of our tainted human nature. The devil does not control our behavior, we actively think, and act for ourselves. However, the devil's influence was established in antiquity. He planted seeds of deceit into the mentality of Adam and Eve, and that seed of disobedience and deceit has spawned generations of people that depend on tainted emotions, self-driven wills and human-centered intellects to make the decisions concerning how they will live and carry themselves through life. Paul the apostle, described his frustrations with trying to live Godly while housed in a body that lacked the power to fulfill his mind's righteous wishes. God made that body but sin originated in a devilish suggestion weakened it.

Flesh does have it's own hang-ups. It wants to do its own thing, and has its own ideas of what works for it and what doesn't. We can't escape that, but we can control it. It's like the mole on your face or the birth-mark or some life long skin blemish that is with you and does not even go away under the application of makeup. It is a permanent resident of your flesh unless you decide to change bodies. But the same way you wear your clothes, and your accessories to cover up the mark, or you do things to make the mark work for your image or you just simply don't think about it, you have to get that kind of mentality with your flesh. There are some habits and some be-haviors that are rooted in your human nature. These have to be dealt with according to their significance and there ability to alter your walk with God. The stuff that needs to be covered until God changes you fully, you cover, not in deception, but through prayer. Paul prayed three times that God would remove the thorn in his flesh but God did not grant him his request He simply was told, "My grace is sufficient for you!" The issue was troubling to Paul but it did not condemn him. It just kept him prayerful, and conscious of his need for God's presence in his life. Then there are the blemishes that actually work for you, and does not cause you to sin but may set you apart as special in the eyes of the world. Always remember that it was God that gave it to you, and that being special is not a bad thing. Last but certainly not least is the stuff you just ignore. We all have stuff we can best just ignore. But when I say ignore I don't mean a callous tossing aside. I mean put it under the blood and leave the rest to God. There's stuff that is completely out of your control and by no magic or manipulation will you ever be able to change it. That's God's business.

The devil is real, I have to reiterate that fact. He is more real than my dark imaginations. He's not my dark side. He's separate from me. He's not the people that seem to be blocking my pathway to destiny although he might be using the difficulty between me and them to make me believe that if I could just get rid of them I will get what I need. He's not our human nature although he played a part in tainting it. He is an entity wholly separate from us. He is to be resisted at every turn. The threat is real but our God and His power is just as real, and in reality is more real. Jesus said it best, "All power has been given unto me in heaven and in earth!" Because of that power there is no weapon that can, will or is formed against them that believe that will prosper.

Essay Three

The Person

"You never forget who you really are.....no matter how many nights you stay awake trying to."

The devil is probably not guilty of the aforementioned quote, but he sure attempts to make us forget who he really is. He keeps us up many nights beating ourselves down, effusively blaming our messy situations on our own weakness. One of the strongest places from which we can address the wrong in our lives, is for us to first assess and acknowledge where we went wrong in the first place. The key is that we must have patience with all things but chiefly have patience with ourselves. We must not lose courage in considering our own imperfections but instantly set about remedying them – everyday we must begin the task anew. Why should we have this constant renewal mindset? Because God has that kind of mindset with regard to us. In considering the person of the devil that idea of constant renewal continuously rings out in my psyche. I have been given ample opportunity to start again but that was not afforded the devil. What kind of person was the devil that God would be so harsh in his handling of his transgression? There are a number of problems that this question uncovers. First, there is the question of, "Can I even consider the devil and what he did within the same terms as what we as humans have done and continue to do?" Then there is the question of, "Should we even question the response of God to the devil's error?" Regardless of where we stand when it comes to the addressing of these questions it is important that we get a better grasp of the person of the devil. The great feat is for us to get pass the persona and get to the real person.

The persona of the devil has been derided by skeptics as so far fetched and outlandish that they have rightly refuted his existence altogether. From the crude to the bizarre has characterized the images that we have developed within the culture to describe the devil. A red-suited, forked-tongue, pointed-ear, mustached denizen that sits diminutively on the shoulder of our enemies and our friends and whispers diabolical orders and suggestions has become the laughingstock of everything from cartoons to sitcoms. We know that this certainly cannot be the image of the person that Jesus spoke about with much more candor than any other New Testament personality connected with the church.

The persona of the devil presented in media and literature and among the cornucopia of popular culture images is a both a poor interpretation and a conspiracy-driven effort by the actual person of the devil to present himself in the most unflattering light so that he can actually gain some twisted compassion from unbelieving humanity. The devil as a person is not the same as he was when he was created by God. From the biblical perspective and worldview, the devil is a fallen angel. He is a created being. Angels according to what we can glean from scripture are beings created prior to man and with faculties that are distinct from man. The debate rages on quietly within Christian scholarship as to whether angels have hypersensitive human attributes. The debate surrounds whether angels have the same at stake emotionally and sensually as human beings. One of the most poignant issues is whether angels have choice and free will like humans do. The interesting thing about the root of these debatable issues is that they all spring from man's quest to make sense of the event that took place in heaven that is accredited with creating the circumstances and reasons why the devil was rejected from heaven and essentially exiled to life in the earth. The facts as the Bible states are that the devil was an angel of great prominence in heaven. The prominence afforded him the creative privilege of being adorned with diadems and carbuncles of priceless value, and being a creature of astounding beauty to behold. According to scripture, not only was the devil awesome to look at, he was also gifted with the ability to produce inspiring music that drove the worship experience in heaven. However, at some point along the way, the devil got beside himself figuratively and began to be in awe of his own self and aspire to sit where God sat. This act showed that this angel in particular had the ability to choose. He chose to, or more correctly intimately desired to be worshipped. He wanted to get the kudos that he was responsible for delivering to God. Does this reflect that angels have a will? It may, but more importantly it gives us insight to the kind of person that God really hates. God hates pride. Pride breeds contempt. The devil's pride was birthed out of his assessment of how "wonderful he was in his own sight." His pride was activated by reason of how phenomenal he had been made by God. His greatness was a result of God's great work, and he lost sight of that. He got caught up with the finished product and forgot about the process, and the one fulfilling the procedure. Let this be a lesson for us, on the way to the top, as we wade out into the depths of faith don't forget who beckoned us out of the boat because we may fall into the devil's snare of self-pride. The person of the devil is most visibly demonstrated in reckless pride.

But the personhood of the devil is not just illustrated in his pride. It is not just reckless, unheralded pride that made God respond in the manner that he did with the devil but it is also the thought the devil didn't leave on his own. He is literally guilty of sedition. Sedition is the divisive illegal act of inciting resistance to lawful authority and tending to cause the disruption or overthrow of the government and in this case it was the government of heaven. The devil sought rebellious company. It is one thing for you to desire to go against God and burn your own path through the fields of resistance but it is another to convince or coerce others to travel with you. It is a sin for you to encourage others to illegal activity just so that you would have company in your crisis. The person of the devil is one that is prideful and teetering toward sedition. Scriptures tells us that a third of the angels followed the devil's erroneous lead. It wasn't that he just arrogantly rebelled against God but he did it while urging others to rebel as well. The Bible says that they lost or forsook their first estate and chose to walk in condemnation.

Thus far we have learned that the bogeyman image of the devil is a far cry from his sinister start. The devil as he stands today was not always evil. Evil and sin was the fruit of his prideful act. Pride was sowed in him and it reaped a harvest of sin and evil. Unfortunately, sin and evil weakens, and that weakening is not just a human deficiency, sin weakens all that touch it. That means that the devil once known simply as Lucifer, the light bearing angel is weakened today to a stature that is far below what he had in heaven because of the sin in him. But never let this understanding of his weakened state fool you into thinking that you can easily take him on. He is weaker than he was at the start but in the arena of the works of the flesh he is formidable because that is his playground. Where the devil plays is where we struggle. Compared to God he is not a match but if he wrestles with us, it is as if he is at play.

Why is the devil powerful in the works of the flesh? Because he is the initiator of fleshly desire. It was the devil through the serpent that enticed Eve to activate the desires of her flesh. It is like the devil wrote the playbook, and he whispered a few plays into Eve's ears, and she tried to run those routes and encourage her husband to run them with her and be-cause of this that attitude was translated to all subsequent generations of mankind. The seeds of sin survived the flood because they were encased in Noah and his children. Although they were in hibernation they survived and as a result recovered to pre-eminence in the culture of man after the subsiding of the flood creating a necessity for the unfolding of the next stage of human redemption which was the arrival of Jesus the Christ in human flesh in the earth.

Just as the seeds of human error were able to hibernate and be passed down from generation to generation, the very nature of the enemy is one that is immersed in an attitude of patience. The devil is patient. Of all his attributes this is the one that can be eradiated in the most positive of lights. Some of us in the faith ironically need to have his level of faith.

The devil has faith in his ability to inundate us with fear and to push us to a place of desperation. He's certainly not of the microwave generation. He is competent in his ability to chip away at the foundations of our faith until the entire structure gives way. After the fall of man with the disobedience of Adam and Eve the devil did not settle for man's failure in the first generation he set his targets on the second generation. He shows up in the lives of Adam and Eve's first children. We see the devil's patience in how he waits for the scent of envy, a close relative of pride, to arise among the second generation of humans. The devil was envious of God. Envy was an accessory of his ornamentation of pride. Therefore when Cain envied the blessing and favor that God showed Abel his brother, the devil burst through the door of his heart and incited Cain to kill Abel. He was patient enough to wait just one more generation to unleash his further attempts to undermine God's mission to populate earth with his replacement-creatures made to worship Him.

Now we have a developing image of the person of the devil, prideful, seditious, and patient. This is the image that depicts him throughout Old Testament scripture. Thus far, we find that none of these descriptors outlines his physique, shape or appearance. This tells us essentially that these elements are not significant at all. Our eyes are the first elements that we use to identify, assess and evaluate the worth and value of things in our life, and unfortunately our eyes are poor measures. They probably are the least reliable of weights on the scales of life. But yet still we sometimes act as if we are slaves to what we see. We determine our attitude based on what we see. We decide whether we will rate the day a great day or a bad day based on what we see. We make plans for our tomorrows based on what we see to-day. And too often we end up in tomorrow and what we saw really did not turn out as we expected. This is the same way we should consider the devil. Pay less attention to what you see that looks to you like devilish ways and be more mindful of what it feels like and what you have learned from scripture to be the real indicators of demonic activity.

It is interesting that none of the devils in the

New Testament gospel accounts of Jesus' are given a physical description. We know that they are devils by what they cause to occur in others. They speak audibly, they make intelligible and intelligent requests of Jesus. They even greet Jesus in the way but never are we given a physical description beyond a cry and an ecstatic response. You should not care how the devil looks. Don't get caught up in how he looks because looks can be distracting. Looks will cause you underestimate his power. Looks may even cause you to get trapped in an ungodly attraction. The person of the devil is crouched not in his appearance but in his personality and character.

Essay Four

The Problem

"The significant problems we face cannot be solved at the same level of thinking we were at when we created them."

-Albert Einstein

What does the devil want to do with us? What is his assignment in my life? For many of us the devil and his ways are manifested in our present situations as problems that we can't get rid of no matter how hard we try. We've employed every strategy that used to work for us and we have come to the humbling conclusion that what worked before does not work now. Our thinking has to develop. We have a problem in this life outside of God, and that problem is the devil. That problem is epitomized in disease, debt, lack, need, addiction, depression and suicidal thoughts. What does the devil really want with us? The discomforts of life like headache, influenza, the common cold and other unavoidable afflictions can give us a sobering comparison by which to really understand what the devil wants with us. All of the aforementioned illnesses have the potential of making our lives miserable. The mildest cases of each may cause us to curtail work and get our schedules out of whack. While the severest cases of each can potentially cause us long term medical issues and at the extreme end death. When it comes to the common cold, influenza, stomach disorders and headaches most of us do not expect death. That seems far fetched. However, when it comes to the devil's agenda it may start out with symptoms that spell one of these minor ailments but the final goal is what we usually consider to be extreme, death, and beyond death our utter destruction and annihilation from the plans and purposes of

God. The devil does not want to just make you sick and cause you to miss time off of work he wants to kill you.

The first time we see or rather, we are alerted to the presence of the devil in the New Testament is at a pivotal time in Jesus' ministry. It is actually right before it is launched. It is in the time of Jesus' greatest physical weakness at the tail-end of a fast and consecration that the devil shows up ready to trap Jesus into some problematic behavior. Just from paying attention to these conditions one can get insight into the problem of dealing with the devil. He attacks not when you are at your greatest strength. He comes when he thinks he can best undermine your progress. Our analysis of our problem or problems should begin at day one when we elicit how we got our selves here in the first place. Was it something I did? Was I in a vulnerable state? Did I have my guard down when I made that poor choice? These are the questions we must ask ourselves as we attempt to assay the problem.

Not only was Jesus hungry and weakened by the fast that had lasted forty days, his flesh may have been anxious to begin the work of ministry, but it was at this juncture that the devil shows up. Never be anxious to start some wonderful pilgrimage or purposeful adventure if you are physically weak, fatigued and hungry. Each of those urgings will overrule your good reason, and your every step will be a battle between fulfilling those fleshly needs and the significance of your calling. But nevertheless, we can glean from Jesus' temptation some wonderful tools to help us fight our urges to fall to temptation even if we are caught in a time of weakness. In the accounts of this exchange between Jesus and the devil in the wilderness, all three of the synoptic gospel writers attempt to lay light on the incident. The first temptation as recorded by each writer was that which accommodated Jesus' most obvious need, the need for food and nourishment. The devil taunted him and said, "If you be the son of God, command that these stones be made bread." The problem with the devil's approach is that it was loaded with assumption and presumption. Just because Jesus had been fasting, he must have this inordinate desire for food. That was what the devil thought. He was wrong. Jesus was hungry but he loved God more. The great problem with most of us is that the devil really wants to test if we love God more than stuff, self or needs. And the further problem is that we unfortunately fail that test question over and over again because we live by the primal needs of our flesh. And because Jesus loved God more He responded to the devil's query with the Word of God. I may be hungry in my flesh, but my spirit man can sustain the rest of me as long as I eat of the Word of God, and do His will.

The second temptation moved from the fulfillment of the flesh, to the fulfillment of prideful attempts to force God's hand. If God really cared for you He would make sure that you won't hurt yourself even if you are being reckless. That was the lie that was entangled in this temptation. If Jesus had done as the devil had wanted he would have been saying He had the right to test or push the boundaries with God, and God was obliged to move. The problem for some of us is that we think that way about God too. We think that we can live anyhow, entertain any kind of thoughts and engage in any sort of behavior and the love of God is obligated to save you from your own acts of suicide. This we know to be untrue. God does not have to intervene and save us from stupid decisions made. Jesus' response was simple I will not tempt God.

The third temptation was about the temptation to take a shortcut to your blessing or destination.

Who wanted more to save mankind? Who wanted more to retain authority in the earth? But gaining this authority by disrespecting God and by subordinating oneself to the will and the way of the devil is not the way we do it. Yes, Jesus' goal was to take possession of the kingdoms of the world but it was so that they would become the kingdoms of our God. God was the end all and the be all of the process of salvation. He was in Christ reconciling the world unto Himself. The devil wanted to thwart God's plans in Christ but he failed and despite the failure as we mentioned earlier he still continued to patiently attempt to delay the fulfillment.

The devil wanted to usurp Jesus' power. He was keenly aware of his assignment in the earth to redeem man unto God. If he could get the Messiah off track, man was as good as doomed. Satan was at his most ruthless during Jesus' ministry because he sensed his impending demise was closer than ever. The Bible says that Jesus came to save man and to destroy the works of the devil. The devil had no chance against Jesus but that was not going to prevent him or cause him to stop his attempts at delaying and destroying us.

In the gospel of Matthew, within the eighth chapter of that book of the Gospels we are informed of a story of two men who were possessed with devils and menaced the country of the Gergesenes. These men were fierce, so fierce that they did not allow any man to pass by that way. This was symptomatic of demonic possession. Again no real description is given for how these devils looked but we are told that they heralded Jesus. "What have we to do with thee, Jesus, thou Son of God? Art thou come hither to torment us before the time?" These are the questions with which the devils accosted Jesus. Demonic possession is accompanied here by violence, and revulsion at the presence of the Son of God. In other demonic episodes the victims were unable to speak, they were blind, experienced seizures, and were engaged in self-destructive behavior. With every incident the devil's recognized Jesus, and the devils were determined to keep humans in bondage.

Our problem is a grave one, and one that we must not take lightly. The devil is ruthless and desires to take no prisoners. He does not just want to see us sick, or drowning in debt, and subdued by worry. He wants us dead. Jesus called the devil a thief. He is a thief that comes to steal, kill and destroy but Jesus came that we might have life and that more abundantly. When we live our lives in such a way that we invite demonic activity by being rebellious, self-willed, disobedient and unbelieving we open up ourselves to death and destruction. Life will remain a fleeting illusion to be pursued but never attained if we think we can find it without Jesus. The devil's greatest scheme has been to convince mankind that he does not exist. Our souls are at stake. We need to make a choice. That choice is belief in Jesus the Christ.

Essay Five

The Solution

"An excuse is worse, and more terrible than a lie, for an excuse is a lie guarded."

-Pope John Paul 1

But Samuel replied, "What is more pleasing to the Lord: your burnt offerings and sacrifices or your obedience to his voice? Listen! Obedience is better than sacrifice, and submission is better than offering the fat of rams. Rebellion is as sinful as witchcraft, and stubbornness as bad as worshiping idols. So because you have rejected the command of the Lord, he has rejected you as King." (1 Samuel 15:22-23)

The answer to defeating the enemy of our souls and defeating the devil is simply to obey God. Throughout my life of faith I have tried to figure out if there was some intricate formula, some system, some procedure that I somehow was missing in the grand scheme of things that would give me victory over the devil and the devilish ways in my life. And as I perused scripture reference after scripture reference the same answer resoundingly came into my spirit, obedience. The only way we can win over the enemy is to obey. We can't skirt pass obedience. We can't avoid following his ordinances. It was disobedience that got us in the mess in the first place and it is obedience that will get us out.

The text of scripture from the book of Samuel is the conclusion of a discourse between King Saul and the prophet and priest of God Samuel. The great charge that the prophet laid on the life of Saul directly from God's mouth was that he had disobeyed. His disobedience had belittled God's directive. His disobedience had led the people of God to disobey God. He had chosen to do his own thing, and to adjust God's decree and that cost him not only his ministry but it cost him his power, and ultimately his life. It was a great injury to God's character for King Saul to go against what God had commanded. King Saul's actions were especially egregious because he disobeyed God before and audience. He was the earthly representative of God standing before the people of Israel. Samuel held the office of priest and prophet, that is true. From the point of view of the Israelites Samuel had direct communication with God. He was God's mouthpiece. But when Saul was established as King he actually took on an earthly position that rightfully belonged to God. The people wanted a king, just like their neighbors. Israel complained to Samuel that they wanted to have a royal representative that would administer justice, govern them and essentially guide them into their destiny. These were all duties that God performed, and for them to ask for a man to take his place was a slight, not of Samuel, but of God. God then proceeded to warn Israel of the dangers of human kings. He told them that in no uncertain terms that absolute power corrupts. He explained to them that their king would eventually tax them. He explained that their labor would be towards benefiting the king. He warned them that their sons and daughters would be taken away from them and made to serve at the kings behest. God told them of all the possible challenges that this request would bring and yet still he granted them their wish.

King Saul at the outset did that which was pleasing in God's sight. He was obedient to God and at one stage the Holy Spirit was upon him so heavily that in a company of prophets he prophesied. But there came a time when Saul decided to disobey God's direct command. And in his disobedience King Saul caused the people of God to also disobey God. His charge was to go against King Agag of the Amalekites and he was supposed to kill everybody and destroy everything, that which was of value and that which was worthless. The Amalekites had inherited a status of indignation in God's book because of how they had treated the Israelites upon their journey across the wilderness into the promise and God demanded their annihilation. But King Saul killed only that which was worthless. He kept everything of value in his eyes and encouraged the people of God to follow suit. He partially obeyed and then he attempted to clean it up by professing that his intention for keeping that which was good, and even sparing the life of King Agag was so that he could offer a sacrifice to the Lord. Little did he understand that if he had killed everything alive as instructed by God he would have been offering the true sacrifice. Sacrifices made within the context of disobedient action aren't sacrifices at all. They are religious rituals that we think can reduce God's retaliatory action against us.

This act of false sacrifice by King Saul is similar to how some of us live transitory lives. I am talking about when it gets easy to recite and recount the wonder of God's grace, the profound power of his restorative Word while we ourselves reside on the fence in our faith, and in our personal lifestyle. We scream repent and deliverance is the way but we are really comfortable living in contradiction. We have managed to be able to shelve our transgressions just long enough to do church work. We sing on the choir, lead praise and worship, have become excellent stewards on the Deacon's Board, but we have personal demons that are constantly reminding us that are lives are fake. We are wrestling with issues that we know speak of a spiritual disconnect. Contemporary Christian news as of late has been filled with story after story of Pastors, para-church organization leaders who have impeccable ministry success and acclaim, but their marriages are a façade and they have some personal hang-ups that can greatly alter and devalue the entirety of their ministry. They know how to sacrifice. They know how to give, but they have problems with being obedient.

It is in our personal wrestling with God over the issues in His word that challenge our proclivities and question our idiosyncrasies, that we get clear direction on what we must declare to be true. A true test of leadership is enduring setbacks while maintaining the ability to show others the way to go forward. Setbacks in the life of a leader are part of the natural course of action in their development as a leader. However, many leaders see setbacks as a sign of failure. They see the setbacks as tragic circumstances rather than therapeutic exercises that teach us about how we should proceed. I believe that leaders that go through God ordained setback fall prey to the devil's insinuations that it is a tragedy, and they will never recover from this, and if this thing ever goes public then their ministry will never reach the heights that they imagine them getting to. Remember the devil is patient. He will manipulate, trouble and disrupt an ungodly issue in you with enough longevity that you don't see it as damaging as it really is, and when believe that you have that issue under control. Then he will maneuver in such a way that when you have reached your height of achievement, and are at the zenith of public view and will pull the sheets off of your scandalous life. The list of victims of this strategy are growing year after year.

Too often the stuff that bothers us spiritually, and in our natural lives that may be besetting sins we avoid even in our personal consecration. The guilt, the feelings of uncleanness, the impure thoughts attached to this issue become the very roadblocks to us getting real deliverance. For some of us, it is because we have tried to casually pray away demonic activity in our lives, and in so doing we unleashed an even more treacherous devilish element that employs aggressive tactics that drives us to push these issues even deeper underground. We are afraid to speak truth that will stick a dagger into the thing that is troublesome to our lives because we are afraid that if that thing dies in us we will never be the same. If I confront that thing, then my ministry will suffer because I depend on that thing to keep me in a posture of desperation-broken and contrite and when I'm under pressure I function better.

It can't be as simple as obedience. Someone is saying that right now. My destiny, my peace, my joy, the rest that I have been pursuing cannot be simply vested in me being obedient to God. As strange, or as simplified as that solution may seem, we can all admit that saying it is easier than walking it out. So we can also agree that obedience is really not that easy, especially if we try to achieve it in our own strength. There's something about us as humans that seems to become especially deficient when we engage the mindset and the purpose of being obedient. As children disobedience seemed so much more an inviting choice. Obedience always appeared a boring choice, lacking adventure. And we learned slowly but surely why obedience was the better choice. Bruises, wounds and tears later we realized that as unexciting as obedience was it was always in our best interest. The entire text of Holy Writ from the Old Testament to the New Testament is a testament of the benefits of slow, deliberate obedience and the contrastingly disadvantageous nature of disobedience. God's unfolding rescue plan for mankind from corruption, sin and death was slow, deliberate but powerfully beneficial. His consequent judgment of disobedience was rather rapid and contagious.

We see obedience win out over sin, sickness and the devil on the cross of Calvary. It was the metaphorical line drawn in the sand of human circumstances that marked the end of useless suffering and sacrifice. When we wrap our minds around what happened on Calvary, and ask ourselves why and how we understand that God is awesome, and as awful as the devil may seem, he lost at his own game on the cross. The end all and be all of demonic activity is death. Jesus died but death had no power over Him. With His death suffering saw its end, sacrifice saw its end, sickness saw its end, disappointment saw its end and Jesus shook these negative attributes off in the grave. Unlike any before, however, Jesus got back up.

Our spiritual minds must get pass Calvary. Not that we forget or forsake the cross but rather that Jesus' suffering and sacrifice becomes a memorial and not a monument in our lives. Let the cross become the cautionary line in our lives that drives us to pursue his glory. See that the cross is a reality and what was accomplished there, releases me from the bondages of sin. My sins past, present and future are nailed to the cross. I've got a choice that they stay there and I march on to a life that is immersed in His Spirit in obedience. Or I can remain walking in circular doubt, pulling sins down from the cross, dabbling in dead things, having only occasional encounters with God but staying undelivered.

We don't have to lie anymore because of the

have overcome the world!" The devil, his demons and the fight for your soul is a fixed fight because God is on your side, obey and reap the benefits of the battle, now and forevermore.

cross. We don't have to cheat anymore. We don't have to be unsettled and uncommitted. We don't have to fear change anymore. Jesus took it on the cross. We lie because we feel that God is not able to get us out of troublesome situations in our lives if we told the truth. But the Bible says, "Who the Son sets free is free indeed." The Bible says, "The truth shall make you free."

We cheat because we feel that God is not able to work for us in spite of the magnified disadvantages that we may be born into, bought our way into, spent our way into or simply fell headlong into. But I've come to declare the Jesus is our kinsman redeemer. He's paid the price. He's given up what is valuable to Him, that we might not get stuck on things that aren't valuable to us at all.

We are fearful of commitment and settling down because we can't trust human kind. But Jesus teaches us there is one that sits high, and looks down low and has greater power than even those in authority over us. He's got the hearts of Kings in his hands. He's concerned about your wellbeing. We are fearful of change because we are too familiar with failure. But know that you are not a failure or a loser. You were born to win. You were born to defeat the enemy. You were made to replace him, that's why you loom so large on his hit list. Don't get depressed when you realize that you are not liked. Know that it comes with the territory. Jesus said, "In this world you shall have tribulation, but be of good cheer for I have overcome the world."

The Devil, his demons and the fight for our souls are topics that we quickly dismiss as being in the background of the Christian struggle. The lore of demonic possession, and his plans and schemes to destroy our lives and at the least, diminish our joy on this side of glory are topics that have been shelved for the more attractive issues of prosperity and Abrahamic wealth. We must understand that our number one problem in this life is not poverty, sickness, disease or immorality. But rather our biggest problem is that the originator of all these issues has cleverly sought ways to "wash his hands" of his involvement in the mess we call life, and some of us have bought into it hook, line and sinker.

We are living defeated lives, scratching and clawing our way through adversity after adversity, because we have failed to address generational assignments of the enemy that it made pass the thin membrane of our mother's birth canal and were implanted into our lives. It all started with him but we have the choice to make sure it ends with us. Uncover them, acknowledge them and annul them under the blood of Jesus Christ.

Hugh J. Harmon is the Senior Pastor of Love Fellowship Kingdom Restoration Tabernacle in Columbia, SC. He is a growing bible scholar, adjunct professor, husband, father of two and mentor to many.

www.ingramcontent.com/pod-product-compliance
Ingram Content Group UK Ltd.
Pitfield, Milton Keynes, MK11 3LW, UK
UKHW020221250726
13967UKWH00001B/126

9 780557 889365